How I cook with spelt

Gabriele Kuppe

AF211102

With this book, I would like to help other people and inspire them to include this valuable grain in their daily diet.

Sincerely,

Gabriele Kuppe

Gabriele Kuppe

How I cook with spelt

Cookbook

imprint

Bibliographic information from the German National Library: The German National Library lists this publication in the Deutsche Nationalbibliografie; detailed bibliographic data can be accessed on the Internet at http://dnb.dnb.de.

© 2022 Gabriele Kuppe

Translation: Gabriele Kuppe

Photos/bookcover: Anna Maria Kuppe and Gabriele Kuppe

Produced and published by: BoD – Books on Demand, Norderstedt (Germany)

English version (German version: Dinkelinspirationen)

ISBN: 978-3-7568-0943-1

Contents

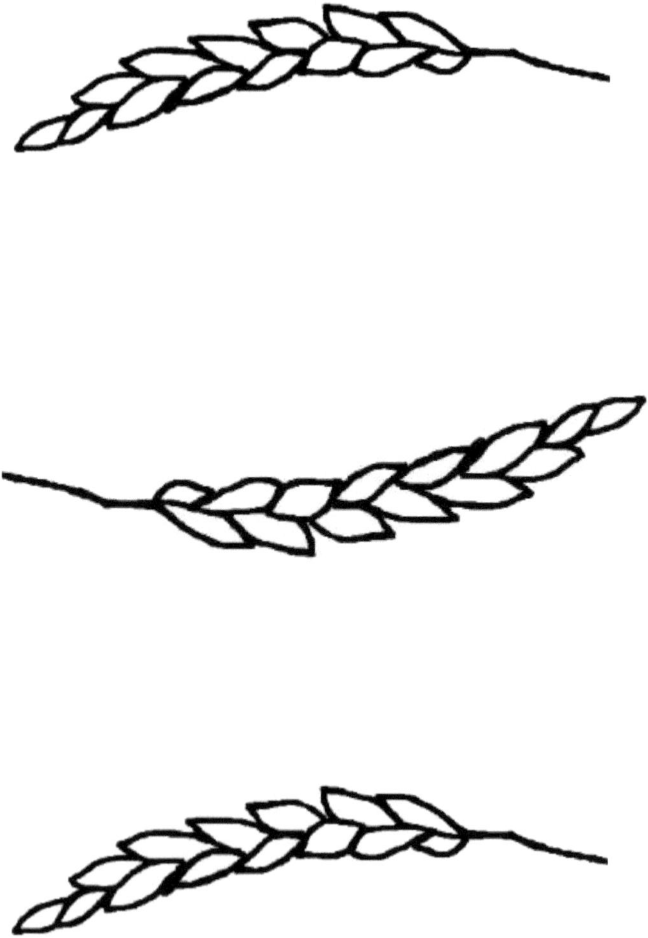

Why spelt?

With all my heart and enthusiasm I can only say:

Spelt made my life easier!

Before I made the decision to switch my diet to spelt, I was often very tired. My body felt partially drained and just quite powerless.

Certainly, the advice I was given from here and there was well intentioned, but I had to learn that not every body reacts the same way. What is good for one person does not necessarily have to be good for another.

I embarked on a journey that, admittedly, was often quite strange and painful. More and more allergies and intestinal problems spread.

It was very clear that I had to change something to feel better again.

"It's all about the food." I have heard this phrase often. Of course, my consumption of sweets was not small. But should that be my problem alone?

Otherwise, I tried a diet here and another option like powders or something similar there. Nothing helped in the long run.

Did I achieve anything with this?

The unequivocal answer to that is: "No." It tends to make you a little more desperate.

The day came when very good friends drew my attention to Hildegard von Bingen. Hmm, who is that?

Research on this lady revealed the following: Hildegard von Bingen was abbess and lived from 1098 -1179. She wrote books in which she passed on her healing knowledge to people. Hildegard von Bingen was a great teacher of her time and spelt was her absolute favorite product.

I read relevant books with interest, for example by Dr. Wighard Strehlow, and found it all exciting and interesting. For me it was clear: I'll try spelt from now on.

Unfortunately this valuable grain has been forgotten for far too long and I'm glad it has been rediscovered.

By eating spelt, I always felt better, was more concentrated and more efficient. That's wonderful! What more did I want?

Of course, I know very well that the first step in changing your diet is not always that easy, after all you are very (sometimes unfortunately too) attached to your old habits.

From my own experience, I can confirm that this decision to include spelt, fruit and vegetables in my diet was the best I have ever made.

Spelt is healthy and really worth including this grain in your life.

For me as a diabetic, it is particularly important that when eating spelt, the sugar digestion is slower and more even than with wheat.

Spelt is a wonderful alternative to other grains.

Typical growing areas are Baden-Württemberg (Germany), Switzerland, Belgium, Finland and Asturias, northern Spain (Escanda) and Central Burgenland in Austria.

Spelt is also valued by farmers because it can be mown dry and is weed-free when harvested. I read that on the website of Stadtmühle Geisingen. There you can, for example, order spelt products online in Germany.

What is perhaps even more interesting is the fact that spelt does not require any chemical fertilizer.

Spelt thrives on barren soil in a harsh climate. What distinguishes spelt is the protective covering, the husk, in which the grain grows, is harvested and stored.

As the very first basis, I recommend soft-boiled spelt grains. This turns the dish into spelt food.

For example, simply fold the spelt grains into a vegetable soup. Of course, this can also be done with any other food.

I recommend doing two teaspoons at a meal, for example at lunch. At first it was a bit annoying because you have to cook the grains fresh every three days. Then the thought comes: "Oh no, now I have to get back to the cooking pot because of these grains!"

But it is - as so often in life - a matter of habit.

Also spelt noodles, spelt flour, spelt flakes, spelt semolina and spelt coffee became my "friends".

Nowadays you can already buy these spelt products in many supermarkets, organic shops, health food stores or order them online. That's no longer a problem.

When baking, however, the cake/pastry is somewhat drier than wheat. But that doesn't matter, it still tastes delicious.

The spelt coffee tastes great. Sometimes the consumption of bean coffee gave me more or less stomach and intestinal problems. With spelt coffee I just felt a pleasure, whether with or without milk and sugar. I didn't mind the "switching" from "normal" coffee to spelt coffee at all.

Even then, I didn't have the feeling that I had to do without anything. This feeling did not occur at all when eating spelt, because this grain is not only healthy but also nutritious.

There are so many wonderful products, such as spelt flakes. They are suitable for morning muesli or desserts.

The spelt noodles are made from spelt flour and the spelt semolina is made like the flour, just a little coarser.

A pudding can be made from spelt semolina or used as an ingredient in cheesecake, for example.

I usually start my day with a spelt flake breakfast or spelt so-called Habermus.

So what`s Habermus?

Habermus consists of spelt groats and spelt grist. I didn't think it would be that tasty at first glance. But that is deceptive. It tastes really good and what is even more important, it has helped me and my intestinal problems superbly.

Just cook a healthy apple with it and it`s complete!

After eating the so-called Habermus I feel full and start the day with a warm meal, Hildegard von Bingen once gave this advice.

It is wonderful that I "found" Hildegard von Bingen.

Over time, I've learned to limit and focus on what I can digest. But, as already mentioned at the beginning, every body reacts differently and so everyone has to find out for themselves whether and what is good for them.

And who does not know the question that one often has to ask oneself. What am I cooking today? It was often quite difficult for me.

Since I think that many other people could experience the same thing as me, I would like to show you, dear readers, below what I cooked and how. It might be a little easier for you then.

Due to many intolerances, I could not simply adopt recipes from books or magazines and had to try out many things.

Feel free to try the recipes below!

Other ingredients such as onions, salt, garlic and much more can be added if required, if you would like to include them in your personal menu.

If there are one or more recipes that already exist, it is really pure coincidence and unintentional.

Let's go to the cooking pots!

Spelt grains

Soft boiled spelt grains

Ingredients:

1 cup of spelt grains (250 ml)

2 cups of water (500 ml)

a pinch of salt

Preparation:

Boil the water and salt. Add the spelt grains and cook slowly over a low heat for about 30 minutes.

Then let it swell for about 60 minutes.

Place the cooled spelt grains in the refrigerator and consume within 3 days.

Spelt Broccoli Casserole

Ingredients for 2 persons:

½ cup of spelt grains (100 grams)

500 grams broccoli

a pinch of salt

1 cup of quark (250 grams)

½ cup of water (100 ml)

2 egg yolks

2 tablespoons mixed herbs

½ cup of goat cheese (150 grams)

Preparation:

Put the spelt grains in a saucepan, cover with water and leave to soak for about 12 hours.

Then bring to a boil, cook over low heat for about 25 minutes.

Wash, clean and cut the broccoli. Bring to a boil in salted water. Cook the broccoli in it for about 8-10 minutes.

Mix the quark with the water and egg yolk. Add the mixed herbs. Season with salt if necessary.

Drain the spelt grains.

Preheat the oven to 375`F (gas mark 5). Grease a casserole dish. Place half of the broccoli in the dish, spread the herb quark over it and sprinkle the spelt grains over it. Place the remaining broccoli on top, and also pour the goat cheese over the mixture.

Bake at 375`F (gas mark 5) for about 20 minutes.

Vegetable soup
with spelt grains

Ingredients for 4 persons:

150 grams of potatoes

150 grams of broccoli

150 grams of carrots

2 cubes of vegetable broth

a pinch of salt

4 cups of water (1 l)

1 - 2 teaspoons cooked spelt grains

Preparation:

Wash, clean, peel and dice the potatoes, broccoli and carrots. Bring to a boil with 1 liter of water.

Then add 2 cubes of vegetable stock and cook for 20-25 minutes.

Mix in 1 - 2 teaspoons of cooked spelled grains and add a little salt if necessary.

Spelt flakes

Spelt flakes
with blueberries

Ingredients:

½ cup of natural yoghurt (150 grams)

1 teaspoon of cinnamon

1 teaspoon of cane sugar

4 heaped tablespoons spelt flakes

1/2 cup of blueberries (125 grams)

Preparation:

Mix natural yoghurt, cinnamon, cane sugar and spelt flakes together.

Add the washed blueberries.

Spelt Flake Muesli

Ingredients:

3 tablespoons dried fruit (mixed)

2 tablespoons spelt flakes

1 small banana

2 tablespoons quark

2 teaspoons of honey or cane sugar

Preparation:

Cut the dried fruit, place in a bowl with water and leave covered in the fridge overnight. Then strain the fruit. Mix the fruit and spelt flakes.

Cut the banana into slices, mix with the quark and honey/cane sugar.

Possibly refine with yoghurt.

Porridge

Ingredients:

4 - 5 tablespoons spelt flakes

1 – 2 teaspoons of cane sugar

1 apple

some water

Preparation:

Slightly boil the spelt flakes in a little water.

Place on a plate and sweeten with cane sugar.

Wash the apple, peel, core, cut into slices and add to the porridge.

If you like, you can also use raspberries, blackberries or other fruit.

Spelt-Habermus

The finished Habermus (without other ingredients such as apple, sugar, sweet chestnut flour and cinnamon) can be obtained from the Stadtmühle Geisingen, for example.

www.stadtmuehle-geisingen.de

Ingredients:

3 heaped tablespoons the so-called spelt Habermus

(from the prepackage)

2/3 cup of water (150 ml)

1 teaspoon of cinnamon

1 sliced apple

1 heaped teaspoon sweet chestnut flour

1 teaspoon cane sugar

Preparation:

Wash the apple, pat dry and cut into slices.

Put the spelt Habermus, apple and water in the pot and let it cook for about 4-5 minutes.

Spelt flake biscuits

Ingredients:

2/3 cup of butter or margarine for baking (150 grams)

2 cups of spelt flakes (200 grams)

½ cup of cane sugar (100 grams)

1 cup of spelt flour (100 grams)

1 teaspoon baking powder

Preparation:

Mix the butter/margarine with the cane sugar and the spelt flakes for baking.

Add the remaining ingredients and mix together.

Form small balls, place on the baking sheet lined with baking paper and press down.

Bake at 350 `F (gas mark 5) for about 12-15 minutes.

Spelt flour

Herb omelet

Ingredients:

½ cup of spelt flour (50 grams)

¾ cup of water (200 ml)

2 eggs

2 tablespoons mixed herbs

A pinch of salt

1 teaspoon of butter

Preparation:

Put the spelt flour, water and eggs in a bowl and stir.

Add the mixed herbs and salt.

Bake thin omelets in a bit butter.

Spelt bread

Ingredients:

4 cups of spelt flour (500 grams)

2 teaspoons of salt

1 tablespoon of apple cider vinegar

1 cube of fresh yeast

4 cups of water (500 ml)

Preparation:

Put the spelt flour and salt in a bowl, mix.

Mix the yeast with 4 cups lukewarm water and add to the spelt flour. Add apple cider vinegar and knead to form a dough.

Line a loaf tin with parchment paper and fill in the batter. Bake in the oven at 400`F (gas mark 6) for about 1 hour.

Spelt bread with apple sauce

Preparation applesauce:

1 apple

A bit water

Cook for 5-10 minutes and mash.

Season with 1 teaspoon cinnamon or cane sugar.

Further ingredients:

2 slices of spelt bread

Possibly 1 teaspoon butter or margarine

Spelt bread with herbs

Ingredients:

1 slice of spelt bread

1/8 cup of cream cheese (30 grams)

1 tomato

3 radishes

Salt

1 tablespoon chives

Preparation:

Spread the spelt bread with cream cheese, wash the tomatoes, radishes and chives and pat dry.

Place the tomato and radishes on the cream cheese bread, season with salt and chives.

Spelt quark rolls

Ingredients:

4 cups spelt flour (500 grams)

1/2 packet of baking powder

2 eggs

2/3 cup of butter or margarine for baking

(150 grams)

2 tablespoons of cane sugar

1 cup of low-fat quark (250 grams)

Salt

2 tablespoons of water

1 egg yolk

Preparation:

Mix the spelt flour with baking powder, eggs, butter/margarine, cane sugar, low-fat quark and a pinch of salt.

Then knead into a smooth dough. Leave covered in the fridge overnight.

Preheat oven to 350 'F (gas mark 5).

Knead the dough briefly again with floured hands, then cut into 12 parts and shape into rolls.

Cover the baking sheet with baking paper. Place the buns on top and cut diagonally.

Mix the egg yolk with water to brush the buns.

Bake at 350 'F (gas mark5) for about 20 minutes.

Potato spelt bread

Ingredients:

4 cups of spelt flour (550 grams)

300 grams of boiled potatoes

1 cube of fresh yeast

2/3 cup of milk (150 ml)

2/3 cup of water (150 ml)

1 teaspoon of salt

Preparation:

Put the yeast in a bowl, salt, leave to stand. The yeast should be liquid.

Then add water and milk (both should be lukewarm) and stir everything together.

Mash the potatoes and add to the yeast mixture.

Fold in the spelt flour. Knead well.

Cover the dough and let it stand until it has expanded.

Knead on a floured surface. Cover with a cloth and leave to stand for another 15 minutes.

Preheat the oven to 400 ꞌF (gas mark 6) and bake the dough for about 20-25 minutes.

Yoghurt spelt bread

Ingredients:

4 cups of spelt flour (500 grams)

2 teaspoons of salt

1 pack of dry yeast

½ tablespoon cane sugar

1 and ½ cup of natural yoghurt (350 grams)

Some butter and flour for the mold

Preparation:

Put the spelt flour, salt, yeast and cane sugar in a bowl and mix together.

Fold in natural yoghurt.

Knead the dough for about 10 minutes.

Cover and let rise in a warm place for about an hour.

Grease a loaf tin and dust with some spelt flour.

Place the dough in the pan, cover again and let it rise for another 30 minutes.

Pre-heat the oven to 400 'F (gas mark 6).

Put the bread in.

After 10 minutes turn down to a bit less than 400 'F (or less than gas mark 6).

Bake another 35 minutes.

Artichoke quiche

Ingredients:

4 eggs

½ cup of cold butter (100 grams)

1 and ½ cup of spelt flour (175 grams)

Salt

2 glasses of artichoke hearts

1 zucchini

2 tablespoons oil

1 cup of cream cheese (200 grams)

Preparation:

Knead butter with 1 egg, spelt flour and some salt.

Line a greased quiche or springform pan (diameter 26 cm) with it and chill for 30 minutes.

Drain the artichokes and quarter.

Wash, trim and dice zucchini.

Heat the oil in a pan, sauté the zucchini for 2-3 minutes, then add the artichokes.

Mix cream cheese and 3 eggs, season with salt.

Spread the vegetables on the dough and pour the egg mixture over them.

Bake the quiche in a preheated oven at 400 ˚F (gas mark 6) on the middle shelf for about 35-40 minutes.

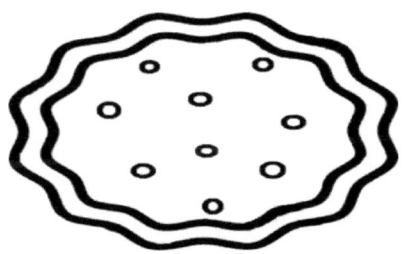

Spelt pizza

Ingredients for 2 people:

1 cup and 2/3 cup of spelt flour (200 grams)

½ packet of baking powder

2/3 cup of quark (150 grams)

2 tablespoons of oil

a pinch of salt

a stick of butter

For covering:

salt, oregano or pizza seasoning

1 cup of goat cheese (100 grams)

Passed tomatoes, salt

Preparation:

Knead spelt flour, baking powder, quark, oil and salt. Grease a pizza pan or round baking dish with butter.

Roll out the dough and place it in the bottom of the pan.

Preheat the oven to 400 'F (gas mark 6).

Rasp cheese.

Season the tomato passata.

Top the dough with tomato passata and a topping of your choice (e.g. tuna, ham, pineapple and more).

Sprinkle the dough with the cheese.

Bake in the oven at 400 'F (gas mark 6) for about 15-20 minutes.

Spelt tarte flambée

Ingredients for 2 people:

2 cups of spelt flour (250 grams)

1 teaspoon of salt

1 tablespoon of oil

2/3 cup of water (150 ml)

2/3 cup of cream cheese (150 grams)

topping of your choice

Preparation:

Mix the spelt flour, salt, water and oil into a smooth dough.

Cover the dough and let it rest for about 30 minutes.

Place the dough on a floured work surface and roll out on the baking sheet.

Occupy by choice.

Bake at 400 ˚F (gas mark 6) for about 12 minutes.

Bright sauce

Ingredients:

2 tablespoons spelt flour

1 tablespoon butter

1 cup of vegetable broth (250 ml)

a pinch of salt

Preparation:

Melt the butter in the saucepan. Stir in the spelt flour with the whisk and deglaze with the vegetable stock. Add salt.

I need this sauce for the vegetable preparation. Simply add broccoli, spinach or carrots, for example.

A delicious vegetable side dish is ready.

Spelt pancakes

Ingredients:

2 cups of spelt flour (250 grams)

2 eggs

2 teaspoons of cane sugar

2 cups of milk (500 ml)

A stick of butter

1-2 apples

Preparation:

Mix spelt flour, eggs and cane sugar and fill with milk until the dough is creamy. Dice or slice the apples and mix into the dough.

Melt butter in the pan and bake the spelt pancakes in batches until golden.

Potato zucchini fritters

Ingredients for 2 people:

4 potatoes

1 zucchini

1 egg

2 tablespoons of spelt flour

a pinch of salt

a stick of butter

Preparation:

Wash the zucchini, pat dry and cut into cubes.

Wash the potatoes, grate finely and mix with the egg, spelt flour and salt.

Pour the mixture into portions in a pan greased with butter and fry until golden brown.

Potato muffins

Ingredients:

2/3 cups of spelt flour (80 grams)

2 tablespoons of cane sugar

3 potatoes

1 teaspoon of baking powder

4 eggs

Preparation:

Boil the potatoes in salted water for about 15-20 minutes until soft. Drain and mash. Put the porridge in a bowl and mix with the spelt flour, cane sugar, baking powder and egg yolk. Beat the egg whites until stiff, add to the mixture. Then pour everything into muffin cups.

Bake in the oven for about 10 minutes at 400 'F. Then switch to 325 'F and bake for another 8-10 minutes.

Allow the muffins to cool or serve warm.

Biscuit cake

Ingredients:

2 eggs

2 cups and 1/3 cup of spelt flour

(300 grams)

1 cup of cane sugar (200 grams)

1 and ½ cup of margarine or butter

(300 grams)

1 teaspoon of baking powder

1 teaspoon of cinnamon

Preparation:

Mix eggs, spelt flour, cane sugar, margarine or butter, baking powder and cinnamon. Knead into a dough.

Pour the batter into a greased and floured loaf tin or small springform pan.

Bake at 350 ʻF for 40 minutes.

Apple fritters

Ingredients:

4 cups of spelt flour (500 grams)

4 cups of low-fat quark (500 grams)

4 cups of butter (500 grams)

a pinch of salt

apple cider vinegar

5 apples

1 tablespoon of cinnamon

Preparation:

For the puff pastry, knead the flour and low-fat quark, add a little bit of apple cider vinegar and salt.

Spread the cold butter in small portions over the mixture and knead. The dough should be smooth.

Then refrigerate for 24 hours.

For the filling, boil the apples and season with cinnamon. Let cool down.

Cut the puff pastry into rectangles and roll out.

Then place the apple filling in the middle of each rectangle, fold over to form apple pockets and press firmly on the edges.

Cut a little at the top.

Bake at 325 °F for about 20 minutes.

Marble cake

Ingredients:

2 cups of butter (250 grams)

1 cup of cane sugar (200 grams)

5 eggs, A pinch of salt

4 cups of spelt flour (500 grams)

1 packet of baking powder

2/3 cup of milk (150 ml)

1 tablespoon of cocoa powder

Preparation:

Cream together the butter, cane sugar and eggs. Mix together the spelt flour, baking powder, salt and milk. Pour 2/3 of the batter into a greased springform pan. Add the cocoa powder and 1 tablespoon of milk to the remaining batter and mix. Put this dark batter on top of the light batter and fold in with a fork. Bake in a preheated oven at 350 'F for 45 minutes.

Spelt Cookies

Ingredients:

2 cups of spelt flour (250 grams)

1 teaspoon of baking powder

½ cup of cane sugar (100 grams)

3 egg yolks

2/3 cup of margarine for baking or butter (150 grams)

Preparation:

Place spelt flour and baking powder in a bowl. Add the egg yolk, margarine or butter and cane sugar and knead into a dough.

Roll out the dough, cut out any shapes you like and bake at 400 ℉ for around 12 minutes.

Chocolate Cookies

Ingredients:

1 cup of butter or margarine for baking (250 grams)

½ cup of cane sugar (100 grams)

1 egg

2 cups of spelt flour (250 grams)

4 tablespoons of baking cocoa

Preparation:

Mix butter/margarine, egg and cane sugar together.

Add the spelt flour and cocoa powder, knead.

Chill in foil for about 30 minutes.

Roll out the dough and cut out with cutters.

Bake at 400 'F for about 12 minutes.

Currant cake
with meringue

Ingredients:

2 cups of currants (300 grams)

½ cup of butter or margarine for baking (125 grams)

3 eggs

1/3 cup of cane sugar (70 grams)

2 cups of spelt flour (220 grams)

1 teaspoon of baking powder

4 tablespoons of milk or water

For the meringue:

1 egg white, ¼ cup of cane sugar (40 g)

Preparation:

Wash the currants and separate from the stalks. Melt the butter and let cool. It should still be lukewarm though. Beat the eggs with the cane sugar until fluffy. Gradually stir in the butter. Mix the spelt flour with the baking powder and milk. Grease the springform pan.

Spread half of the batter in the springform pan, place half of the currants on top. Put the rest of the dough on top and top with the remaining currants.

Bake in a preheated oven at 350 °F for about 10 minutes.

Meanwhile, for the meringue, beat the egg whites until stiff. Add the cane sugar and fold in. Spread the meringue over the cake. Then put back in the oven and bake for another 15 minutes.

The meringue should be browned. Let cool down.

Strawberry tart

Ingredients:

2 and ½ cup of spelt flour (300 grams)

1 and ½ cup of strawberries (250 grams)

2/3 cup of butter or margarine (150g)

3 tablespoons of cane sugar

2 eggs

1 teaspoon of baking powder

Preparation:

Knead all the ingredients and leave to rest in the fridge for half an hour.

Divide the batter into small tart molds that have been greased beforehand.

Bake in a preheated oven at 325 'F for about 20 minutes.

Let cool down. Then place the strawberries on top and cover with cake glaze (see respective packaging for preparation).

Apple muffins

Ingredients:

1 and 2/3 cup of spelt flour (200 grams)

2 teaspoons of baking powder

½ cup of cane sugar (100 grams)

½ cup of butter (100 grams)

2 apples

2 egg yolks

½ cup of milk or water (100 ml)

Preparation:

Mix all ingredients together to form a dough.
Distribute in muffin molds and bake at 350 ℉ for about 25 minutes.

Berry Slices

Ingredients:

2/3 cup of butter or margarine (150 g)

1 cup of cane sugar (200 grams)

2 eggs

1 and ½ cup of spelt flour (175 grams)

2 teaspoons of baking powder

½ cup of milk (100 ml)

1 and 1/3 cup of raspberries (200 g)

1 cup of blackberries (150 grams)

1 tablespoon of cornstarch

3 egg whites

Preparation:

Preheat the oven to 350 'F. Line a high baking tray with parchment paper.
For the dough, cream the butter/margarine and ½ cup of cane sugar (100 grams). Fold in eggs one at a time. Mix spelt flour with baking powder. Stir the mixture into the batter, alternating with the milk. Spread the dough onto the sheet. Bake on the middle shelf for about 25 minutes.

Wash the berries, heat. Mix the water and cornstarch until smooth, stir into the berries, simmer until a compote is formed. Remove the cake from the oven, increase the temperature to 425 'F.
Spread the compote over the dough.
For a meringue, beat the egg whites until stiff and sprinkle in ½ cup of cane sugar (100 grams). Spread the whipped cream over the berries.
Let the cake bake for about another 10 minutes.
Remove, let cool and divide into slices.

Cream puff
with raspberry cream

Ingredients:

¼ cup of butter or margarine for baking
(50 grams)

Salt

1 cup and ¼ cup of spelt flour (150g)

4 eggs

1 and 1/3 cup of raspberries (200 grams)

1 and ½ cup of cream (400 grams)

2 tablespoons of cane sugar

1 cup of water (250 ml)

1 pack of cream stabilizer

Preparation:

Boil the butter/margarine with 1 cup of water (250 ml) and a little salt in a saucepan. Add the spelt flour and stir until the mixture comes off the bottom of the pan like a lump. Place this choux pastry in a bowl and let cool.

Stir the eggs into the choux pastry and place in a piping bag.

Preheat oven to 425 ℉.

Pipe the choux pastry onto a baking sheet. Then bake for 20-25 minutes. After removing, cut off a lid and leave to cool.
Wash the raspberries.
Whip the cream with the cane sugar and cream stabilizer until stiff. Place in a piping bag.
Fill the bottom halves with cream and raspberries.

Put the lid on.

Cinnamon summit

Ingredients:

2/3 cup of butter or margarine for baking
(150 grams)
2 cups of spelt flour (250 grams)
2 teaspoons of cinnamon
2 egg yolks
1 and ¼ cup of cane sugar (150 grams)

Preparation:
Mix all ingredients together.
Place the dough in the fridge for about 1
hour.
Then roll out and shape into small rolls.
The cookies at 350 ℉ for about 12
minutes to bake.

Spelt pasta

Spelt spaghetti with vegetable sauce

Ingredients:

3 cups of spelt spaghetti (250 grams)

4 cups of water (1 Liter)

1 tomato

1 zucchini

1 stick of butter

1 tablespoon of tomato paste

½ and 1/3 cup of vegetable broth (200 ml)

a pinch of salt

Preparation:

Wash tomatoes and zucchini and cut into small cubes.
Melt a piece of butter in the pan and let the vegetables simmer for about 5 minutes.
Then add 1 tbsp tomato paste and simmer for about 1 minute.
Pour in the vegetable stock and simmer for about 10 minutes.
Finally add a pinch of salt.
Cook the spelt spaghetti according to the instructions.

Spelt pasta
with Herb butter

Ingredients:

3 cups (250 grams) of spelt pasta
(spaghetti, linguine)

4 cups of water (1 Liter)

Salt

1 cup of butter (250 grams)

2 teaspoons mixed herbs

Preparation:

Boil spelt noodles in salted water.
Cream the butter, add salt and fold in the
mixed herbs.
Serve together.

Spelt pasta salad with herbs

Ingredients for 4 persons:

3 cups of spelt pasta (250 grams)
1 zucchini
1 cup of cocktail tomatoes (125 grams)
Salt

For the dressing:
2 tablespoons of oil
2 tablespoons of mixed herbs

Preparation:

Cook the spelt noodles in boiling water according to the packaging instructions and drain.
Mix together the ingredients for the dressing.
Mix the zucchini, tomatoes, spelt pasta and dressing together.

Spelt pasta salad with ham

Ingredients for 3 people:

3 cups of spelt pasta (250 grams)

A pinch of salt

3 dill pickles

200 grams of beef ham or poultry meat sausage

250 grams of salad cream

Preparation:

Boil spelt noodles in salted water.
Cut the ham/poultry sausage into strips.
Mix the spelled noodles, the dill pickles, the ham/poultry sausage and the salad cream, season with salt.

Spelt noodle soup

Ingredients for 2 people:

2 cups of soup spelt noodles (200 grams)
A pinch of salt
1 teaspoon of butter
2 cups of vegetable broth (500 ml)

Preparation:

Bring salted water to a boil. Cook the
spelt noodles in it until al dente, drain
and drain.
Pour in the vegetable stock (see package
instructions) and simmer over low heat
for about 10 minutes.
Add the spelt noodles and serve.

Spelt spaetzle with beans

Ingredients for 2 people:

2 cups of spelt spaetzle (200 grams)

500 grams of snap beans from the refrigeration

250 grams of chicken breast fillet

2 cups of cream cheese (200 grams)

1 cup of vegetable broth (250 ml)

200 grams of mushrooms

A pinch of salt

2 teaspoons of mixed herbs

A stick of butter

Preparation:

Boil the beans in salted water.
Cook the spelt spaetzle in salted water according to the packaging instructions and drain.
Wash and clean the mushrooms, cut into small pieces.
Wash the chicken breast fillet, pat dry and cut into pieces.
Put some butter in a pan and briefly fry the chicken breast fillet in it, salt and set aside.
Now add the mushrooms, beans and spelled spaetzle to the pan and stir.
Add the cream cheese, herbs and some vegetable stock to the mix in the pan and mix.

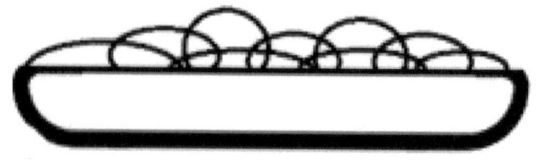

Spelt pasta
in tuna sauce

Ingredients for 2 people:

2 cups of spelt pasta (200 grams)
A pinch of salt
1 can of tuna natural
100 grams of sun-dried tomatoes in oil

Preparation:

Cook the spelt noodles in boiling salted
water according to the packaging
instructions.
Drain tuna, drain.
Drain the tomatoes, reserving the oil and
set aside.
Wash tomatoes, cut into pieces.
Add the tuna, tomatoes and 2
tablespoons of tomato oil (or other oil),
heat everything while stirring. Season the
sauce with salt.
Serve with the noodles.

Spelt semolina

Spelt semolina soup

Ingredients:

A stick of butter

5 tablespoons of spelt semolina

4 cups of water (1 Liter)

2 vegetable bouillon cubes

Salt if necessary

Preparation:

Melt the butter in a saucepan, add the spelt semolina and stir, pour in 4 cups of water, add stock cubes and simmer for 5 minutes.

If necessary, the soup can be seasoned with a little salt.

Spelt semolina porridge

Ingredients for 2 servings:

2 cups of milk (500 ml)
2 tablespoons of butter
2 tablespoons of cane sugar
3 tablespoons of spelt semolina (75 grams)

Preparation:

Bring the milk, butter and cane sugar to a boil. Stir in the spelt semolina, bring to the boil while stirring.
Simmer over low heat.

Small Cheesecake

Ingredients:
3 eggs
½ cup of butter (90 grams)
1 cup of cane sugar (200 grams)
3 cups of low-fat quark (750 grams)
2 tablespoons of spelt semolina (50g)
½ teaspoon of baking powder

Preparation:
Separate the eggs. Beat the egg whites
and set aside. Cream the egg yolks with
the butter and cane sugar. Gradually stir
in the low-fat quark, spelt semolina and
baking powder. Fold in the egg white.
Pour the batter into a springform pan
(diameter 20 cm) lined with baking paper.
Bake in the oven at 425'F for 15 minutes.
Then change the temperature to 350 'F
and bake for another 50 minutes.

Spelt semolina dumpling soup

Ingredients for 2 people:

3 cups of vegetable stock (750 ml)
¼ cup of butter (50 grams)
1 egg
4 tablespoons of spelt semolina (85g)
Salt

Preparation:
Heat the vegetable broth.
Cream the butter. Gradually add the egg
to the butter and let the spelt semolina
trickle in. Season with salt.
Using two teaspoons, cut out small
dumplings from this mass and add to the
slightly boiling vegetable broth.
Let it steep for about 15 minutes.

Recipe directory

Artichoke quiche -40-

Spelt pizza -42-

Spelt tarte flambée -44-

Bright sauce -45-

Spelt pancakes -46-

Potato zucchini fritters -48-

Potato muffins -49-

Biscuit cake -50-

Apple fritters -52-

Marble cake -54-

Spelt cookies -55-

Chocolate cookies -56-

Currant cake with meringue -57-

Strawberry tart -59-

Apple muffins -60-

Berry slices -61-

Cream puff with raspberry cream -63-

Cinnamon summit -65-

Spelt spaghetti with vegetable sauce -67-

Spelt pasta with Herb butter -69-

Spelt pasta salad with herbs -70-

Spelt pasta salad with ham -71-

Spelt noodle soup -72-

Spelt spaetzle with beans -73-

Spelt pasta in tuna sauce -75-

Spelt semolina soup -77-

Spelt semolina porridge -78-

Small cheesecake -79-

Spelt semolina dumpling soup -81-

Sources of supply

Stadtmühle Geisingen
Mühlenweg 11
78187 Geisingen (Germany)

Tel: (07704) 9241-0
www.stadtmuehle-geisingen.de

Dr. Wighard Strehlow

Strandweg 1

78476 Allensbach (Germany)

Book: Die Ernährungstherapie der Hildegard
von Bingen, Knaur Verlag

www.virita.de

https://de.wikipedia.org/wiki/Dinkel

Units

I researched the units of measurement on various sits on Pinterest and google.

For example at:

www.pinterest.de

www. Google.de

www.biteitquick.com

Freche Freunde (pinterest)

www.simply-yummy.de

www.backenmachtgluecklich.de

WiegenohneWaage (pinterest)

Flour

1 cup = 125 grams

½ cup = 62 grams

1/3 cup = 42 grams

¼ cup = 31 grams

1 tablespoon = 8 grams

Sugar

1 cup = 200 grams

½ cup = 100 grams

1/3 cup = 67 grams

¼ cup = 50 grams

1 tablespoon = 12 grams

Butter

1 cup = 227 grams

½ cup = 83 grams

1/3 cup = 75 grams

¼ cup = 57 grams

1 tablespoon = 14 grams

Milk, Water, Oil

1 cup = 240 ml (Milliliter)

½ cup = 120 ml

1/3 cup = 80 ml

¼ cup = 60 ml

1 tablespoon = 15 ml

Dairy products, cream, yoghurt, curd

1 cup = 240 grams

½ cup = 120 grams

1/3 cup = 80 grams

¼ cup = 60 grams

Grains

1 cup = 128 grams

½ cup = 64 grams

1/3 cup = 43 grams

Flakes

1 cup = 100 grams

½ cup = 50 grams

1/3 cup = 35 grams

¼ cup = 25 grams

Temperatures

275 'F = 140 degrees Celsius

300 `F = 150 degrees C.

325 'F = 165 degrees C.

350 'F = 180 degrees C.

375 'F = 190 degrees C.

400 'F = 200 degrees C.

425 'F = 220 degrees C.

450 'F = 230 degrees C.

Noodles

1 Cup = 90 grams

½ cup = 45 grams

1/3 cup = 30 grams

¼ cup = 20 grams

1/8 cup = 10 grams

Tablespoons

1 tablespoon flour = 20 grams

1 tablespoon sugar = 25 grams

1 tablespoon semolina = 20 grams

1 tablespoon oil = 15 grams

1 tablespoon butter = 20 grams

1 tablespoon honey = 25 grams

8 tablespoons water/milk = 1/8 Liter or 125 grams

Dear readers,

The information and advice contained in this book has been carefully selected. Nevertheless, all information is without guarantee.

The author and the publisher cannot accept any liability for any disadvantages or damage resulting from the practical information given in the book.

Each application is at the user's own risk and responsibility.

If necessary, please seek medical advice or ask your non-medical practitioner.

Wish you a lot of success.

Biography of the author

Gabriele Kuppe was born in the Rhineland. She grew up in the Ruhr area, went to school there and since 1978 her life has been back in the Rhineland.

As a child, she liked to write stories, which remained unpublished. Other hobbies are music and dancing.

However, her path initially steered in a completely different direction. After graduating from high school, Gabriele Kuppe worked by a lawyer for a number of years until she started working as a typist and later as a customer advisor in a mortgage bank.

The author has been writing books since 2011 and she wants to encourage and inspire other people.

Notes